ADJUSTING TO LIFE IN AMERICA

The Ultimate Guide: What You Need to Know

JOE K. MUNGAI, MSW, LISW

ADJUSTING TO LIFE IN AMERICA

The Ultimate Guide: What You Need to Know

Copyright 2020 © Joe K. Mungai, MSW, LISW

Joe K. Mungai, MSW, LISW

2150 James St # 5204 Coralville IA 52241

Email: info@thesimpleinsights.com

Website: www.thesimpleinsights.com

All rights reserved. No part of this eBook or program in general may be reproduced or transmitted in any form or by any means, electronic or mechanical, including photocopying, recording, or by any information storage and/or retrieval system, without the express written consent of the publisher, Joe K. Mungai, and/or their legally delegated representative(s). This publication contains the opinions and ideas of the author. It is intended to provide helpful and informative material on the subjects addressed in this publication. It is provided with the understanding that the author and publisher are not engaged in rendering medical, health, psychological, or any other kind of professional and consulting services in the publication. If the reader requires personal medical, health, or other assistance or advice, a competent professional should be consulted. The author and publisher specifically disclaim all responsibility for any liability, loss, or risk, personal or otherwise, that is incurred as a consequence, directly or indirectly, of the use and application of any of the contents of this guide, and/or of this entire program in total.

TABLE OF CONTENTS

PREFACE

Why You Should Read This Book

"Learn how to use the experience of others to succeed and thrive using their strategies. Why re-invent the wheel if it's working?" – Joe Mungai

I wrote this book to help you with your adjusting process in America, especially if you are new. I want you to have a good start in your journey of integration. But more than that, I want you to have a better outcome. This is in line with my passion of helping others as they navigate new cultures, environment and systems. And so I have made it my goal to help make your acculturating in America less complicated. Part of this involves reflecting on my own journey of acculturation in America so as to share with you what I now know, that I didn't know, when I was new in America. The knowledge I share with you in this book has contributed immensely to my personal success in America. I will also share with you some important nuggets of wisdom that other immigrants have discovered in the course of their immigration journey. My aim in sharing and passing on this important information is to help make your life easier while you are settling down in the United States of America. This is my contribution in helping you as you battle what I call **"The Beast of Integration."**

There are lots of things that I now know and which I have included in this book that make me say, "I wish I had such a manual upon arrival." But then, I wouldn't have discovered what I have discovered and what I'm sharing with you now.

You can tell how strongly I feel about this topic; I felt compelled to compile and publish this book to help you adjust to life in America. I tell all my students that, "You shouldn't re-invent the wheel if it's not broken." I encourage them to learn how to use the experience of others to succeed and thrive using their strategies.

My mission in writing this book is to broaden your experience and help you learn not only from my own experience, but also from the experiences of other immigrants who landed here before you.

I have lived in America for more than fifteen years, and in the course of that time I have discovered the importance of quickly learning the ins-and-outs of the host culture. As you know, learning never stops. You pick up new ideas and information as you progress in life. This book will not provide you with all the information you need, but it will give you a good starting point and a structure as you lay your foundation. I personally make effort to learn something new every day; I hope that you will learn to do the same for yourself. It's a good practice to adopt, and it has amazing outcomes.

Part of the acculturation process in your host country means adjusting bit-by-bit and balancing your new culture with the culture you have always known. What this means, is that you will find yourself keeping some part of your old culture at the back of your mind as you learn and acquire what you need to know in your new culture. This realization gets more grounded in me with every passing year. It took a while, but I came to this realization that you cannot live a full life in your host country without learning parts of your new culture. You can still hold onto parts of your original culture, values and traditions while on this journey. As you progress, I want you to know that it's not a betrayal of your parents or family if your new culture becomes more manifested in your life than some parts of your original identity as you take in elements of your host country's culture. I say this with a lot of respect for your culture, being one who has been here, and has done it.

The other thing that I have realized, which is a major reason I put this book together is that:

The greatest source of suffering for most immigrants while in the US is lack of access to relevant and helpful information to help them improve the quality of their life. And for those with access to that information, their main undoing is failure to take advantage of it. Those two reasons explain the suffering of the majority of immigrants in the U.S.

This is why I tell my students: *"The biggest reason for your lack of thriving in America is not other people or the systems no matter how complicated they might be, as many will have you believe; it is most likely you. Most likely, you are the one who fails to take responsibility to make good things happen to you, your family and your community."*

There are those who will not ask for help, even when the help is right there, when they desperately need it. If you ever need help, ask for it. Americans are big-hearted and are very likely to help someone in need. The initial period of adjustment is very tough, so don't be ashamed to ask for help. You will make it through; we all did. But it's much easier if you get some help along the way.

One thing I suggest you start early is: devote at least one hour daily, seven days weekly, three hundred and sixty-five days annually – including all Sundays and holidays – to study and train for a better job.

If you are working for an industrial or agricultural corporation for example, ask to be allowed to help in repair shops, etc. during your off days – even for a few hours after working in the fields – without pay, just to learn and train. That expression of ambition and willingness to make an investment will catch the attention of the managers.

Also, don't be lazy in improving your spoken English. Language is important. It's ok to speak with an accent. However, it's **NOT** ok not to speak English. Not speaking English will disadvantage you severely. You will have to learn it eventually, but you'll dearly wish you had learnt it earlier. Get school going immigrant children teach you how to speak English, watch children's TV with them, ask them to translate the dialogue. You can also join English language learner conversation groups or enroll for an English class to improve your English-speaking skills. You will be glad later if you do this now. I am sure you will reach out to thank me eventually for sharing this with you.

We are far from being done talking about improving English-speaking skills. This subject has been close to my heart. We will revisit it again later in this book. I'm going to show you more opportunities that are available to help you develop your skills in this area. I also want you to learn from the experiences of other immigrants as I share their observations later on in this book.

I sincerely hope that what I share in this book will be relevant enough to make a difference in your life.

FOREWORD

It is my great pleasure to write this foreword.

ADJUSTING TO LIFE IN AMERICA, by Joe Mungai, is a timely resource that will provide much needed guidance to immigrants and members of refugee community as they adjust to life in America.

I have had the opportunity to personally observe Mr. Mungai as a court interpreter as he helps bridge the communication gap between non-English speaking individuals and the other people involved in the court system.

The justice system is complex and intimidating, even to those who have grown up around it. For non-English speakers, in particular, there is a myriad of other challenges they need help to navigate. Mr. Mungai's input is this area has been essential to our system. He helps facilitate communication with the court in a professional manner while still being a friendly and compassionate individual to those he assists. Without his input, the court system would not be efficient. His work is highly valuable to the people that the justice system exists to serve.

His desire to expand his work through this book is noteworthy. It's my hope that many will benefit from his work and service.

Honorable Jason A. Burns

Judge, Sixth Judicial District of Iowa

INTRODUCTION

"Don't wish it was easier, wish you were better. Don't wish for less problems, wish for more skills. Don't wish for less challenge, wish for more wisdom."
– Jim Rohn

There are specific resources and supports you need to have in order to succeed in America. Many immigrants and members of the refuge community don't know about these resources and supports, or where to find them. It's even more difficult for those who are new in America and don't know where to start or what to do to succeed. Good news; you don't have to go through this experience alone just because others before you went through the same. This book is the ultimate guide to the success of immigrants in America. Whether you are a new immigrant, or you have been in the U.S. for a while, you will learn valuable lessons from shared experiences.

In this book, I share with you the most important information you need as you settle in America. You'll get both the knowledge of the resources you need, and practical guidelines of where to find those important resources, services and supports. I am glad to let you know that the information you need in your journey to integration in America is available and accessible to you.

First, I'll help you to discover the resources that are important in the many areas of your life in America. Then, I'll show you how to make use of that knowledge as I guide you on how to take advantage of the opportunities available for your own benefit, your family and your community. This is because when you thrive, your community thrives, and everyone is happy.

So, who am I?

I am your partner for your success in America. For almost two decades, I have worked in the social service field in the USA as a social worker while at the same time interacting and orienting new immigrants to the U.S. and getting a kind of continuing education myself during that time. I have been learning about immigrants' hopes and fears, how they build their lives or destroy them, and why either of the two happens. One thing that has been clear throughout my experience is the fact that the same information that many Americans need to succeed is very much what immigrants also need to succeed in their new country. Some of the greatest barriers that immigrants must overcome in order to achieve success in America is lack of knowledge of resources they need, knowing where to find them, and the skills to access them, as I had alluded to earlier. They also need to gather enough courage to take advantage of these resources after acquiring knowledge of their existence. That realization started the process that resulted into this book and also changed the way I define what I do. I now view all my work with immigrants and refugee community as a practice supporting their success, well-being and growth by educating them on available resources in the U.S. and how to access them.

I have written this book to pass that information to you. I have presented and shared the same knowledge with so many others face-to-face and through various other methods of communication. The results were phenomenal after this knowledge was put into practice.

I hope and believe that the ideas in this book will make a meaningful and lasting difference in the quality of your life.

CHAPTER 1

ADJUSTING TO LIFE IN AMERICA

"Helping immigrants battle the beast of integration benefits everyone."
– Joe Mungai

I never knew adjusting to U.S culture would be that difficult!

I often hear that statement from immigrants. *"As much as I had prepared to adjust to Life in the U.S., I never knew it was going to be that difficult."*

That's why you need to learn now and get help with your own adjusting.

I came across great information on the subject of adjusting to life in U.S. that was shared by Vanderbilt University through their communication division which I found helpful and I adopted for the purpose of this section. I want to share it with you. I hope that you will find it helpful too. They explain very well the process of adjustment to life in the U.S. and they address issues such as:

- How to Adjust to Life in the U.S.
- Stages of Adjustment
- Where to Find Help When its Needed
- Understanding U.S. Culture, Customs and Social Interactions

Culture, Customs and Social Interactions

As a new immigrant or a member of refuge community who has just joined a new culture and a new community in the U.S., it's normal to feel overwhelmed, excited, nervous, sad, frustrated, happy, and a lot more – all at once, as you transition to life in the United States. I still recall how home-sick and overwhelmed I felt when I was new in America after moving away from friends, family, and the familiarity of home. The start of my journey in this country challenged me both in a positive and negative way. I share with you this experience, because I want you to know that you are not alone. Do not be alarmed or surprised if you find yourself feeling confused, frustrated or lonely after your big move, or as you adjust to life in the United States. Later on, towards the end of the book I will share with you some of the things I did to help myself and others who were experiencing the same difficult feelings I was experiencing when I was new in America. But allow me to share some suggestions with you that you can start utilizing right away if needed.

There are several places in your community where you can seek help and support if you are feeling lonely. A good place to start (depending on your interest) is reaching out to your local church or religious organization so you can find fellowship through their small groups, which can put you in connection with others. Meditation and spiritual inspiration have also been found to help people deal with loneliness. Also, if you contact your local library, you can also get a list of nearby places in your community where you can seek help and support by speaking to a mental health professional (counselor) who will guide you on how to manage your feelings of loneliness and develop healthy coping skills as needed. This is important, especially if those feelings are overwhelming and affecting your daily life. If you are a student, these services are offered for free at your school, and the information will be kept private by your provider. These services are also offered in a confidential manner at your work place. A trained local church pastor might also offer some support to you and to your family in this area.

Cultural Adjustment Stages

It has been said that adapting to a new culture is a continual process that lasts throughout one's life-time. Understanding the adjustment process helps not only immigrants but also U.S. citizens to accept the cultural differences and the occasional feelings of alienation and frustration that come with it.

In most situations in life, knowing what to expect and in this case understanding the adjustment process ahead of time helps you to know:

How to prepare;

What to look for; and hopefully,

What to do.

Knowing what to expect is supposed to help you feel a little more in control of the situation.

As part of the preparation process, you need to know the following four stages of cultural adjustment:

1. *Honeymoon*
2. *Culture shock (Hostility)*
3. *Adjustment (humor)*
4. *Mastery: At Home*

HONEYMOON: Exhilaration and anticipation characterize the

"Honeymoon Stage," during which immigrants are generally fascinated with all that is new and are open to meeting new people and experiencing new things. However, their enthusiasm to please their hosts may make them nod or smile to indicate understanding when in fact, they have not truly understood what is being said or done. That leads to misunderstandings, and when misunderstandings build, immigrants are likely to experience the second stage of cultural adjustment.

HOSTILITY: Frustration, anger, anxiety, and sometimes depression take over during the *"Hostility Stage."* The initial excitement is replaced by frustration because of bureaucracy, the difficulty of navigating new complicated systems and the weariness of speaking and listening to talk communicated in English. At this point, many immigrants may display hostility toward people of the new culture. Minor frustrations may lead to fear, mistrust, and lack of interest in the new culture.

HUMOR: The *"Humor Stage"* follows when the immigrants begin to relax in the new culture and to laugh at the minor mistakes and misunderstandings that previously caused them headaches. This often occurs after an immigrant has gained friends, is able to figure out and to manage the new environment.

HOME: The *"Home Stage"* occurs when the immigrant "feels at home" in the new culture while still retaining allegiance to his or her native culture. Thus, the immigrant gains the ability to live successfully in two cultures.

Adopted from Vanderbilt University Division of Communication on Adjusting to Life in the U.S.

CHAPTER 2

UNDERSTANDING U.S. CULTURE & CUSTOMS

"Finding is reserved for those who search." - Jim Rohn

I never knew, that when an American smiles and says, *"Nice to see you,"* it doesn't necessarily mean that he/she is truly glad to see me.

Many immigrants get thrown off balance by this behavior from majority of Americans, whose words don't seem to necessarily match their actions in this area. By saying, *nice to meet you,* the Americans are probably just being polite. I have learned, and so have many other immigrants, that in general, Americans are, more often than not, very friendly, approachable and helpful. But you want to be careful not to equate that with wanting to be friends.

Many immigrants and members of refugee community have a notion that Americans are superficial and that their friendship follows a pattern of *"too much, too soon, and not enough time given."* But, just as everywhere else, becoming good friends with someone takes time. This is what I have observed in many cultures, and in this culture, the same appears to be true.

Here are few more things I've learnt from experience about U.S. customs which could help you.

GREETING PEOPLE

I want to bring this to your attention; **"Informal"** often describes social and even professional life in the U.S. First names are often used. However, during initial introductions, and in formal or business situations, it is better to address someone as Dr., Mr., Mrs., or Ms., than by first name if invited to do so. For example, when I was in college, I learned that students here in America generally use first names with peers and last names with professors. *"Hello"* and *"How are you"* are common greetings. *"How are you"* is more of a social convention than a genuine desire to hear about another person's well-being. In addition to a verbal *"Hello"* or *"Nice to meet you,"* a handshake is a standard form of greeting for both men and women.

PERSONAL SPACE & ETIQUETTE

It's important to know that, in the U.S., people lend considerable space between themselves and others. If a person backs away during a close conversation, the person is likely trying to reestablish a comfortable personal distance. I also want you to be aware, that people in the U.S. are concerned with personal cleanliness, bathe frequently and use a lot of soap and deodorant, but rarely cologne. Although this might seem exaggerated by other cultural standpoints, attention to personal hygiene is important for business and social success in the U.S.

TIME ORIENTATION

it's important to know that despite an emphasis on informality, **punctuality is valued**. Meetings, social functions, classes, scheduled work time, shifts and other organized activities start within minutes of the established time. This applies to professional appointments as well as dinner with friends.

Social Interaction & Visits

Casual acquaintances are easily made and easily lost. And as I said earlier, close friendships result from repeated interaction between people and the sharing of mutual interests and activities. The key is to participate in informal conversations, without letting insecurities of language ability prevent an attempt at friendship. Informal social invitations can be easily misunderstood. People will occasionally say, *"Stop by sometime,"* or *"Let's get together,"* as a polite way of saying, *"Good-bye."* This is more a form of speech than an invitation. However, either of the individuals may initiate a closer friendship by calling to arrange a get-together.

Host gifts, such as flowers or a memento from one's home country, are appreciated but are not necessary. And in regard to meals, the host should be informed in advance of any dietary restrictions. It is acceptable to ask if anything contains ingredients that one cannot eat.

Adopted from Vanderbilt University Division of Communication on Adjusting to Life in the U.S.

CHAPTER 3

CHALLENGES FACING IMMIGRANT PARENTS AND THEIR CHILDREN

"The greatest gift you can give your children are the roots of responsibility and the wings of independence." – Denis Waitely

Immigrant families to the United States can face many challenges, complicating their adjustment to the new host culture.

I share here below an article that I adopted that was put together by a fellow social worker based in Canada, which I found to have helpful practical suggestions especially to parents as they raise their children in a new foreign culture.

When new immigrant and refugee families move to America, often unconsidered is the implications for intra-familial culture clash when children take to the host culture sooner or more wholeheartedly than their parents. Risk of conflict between children and their parents is heightened on issues of socialization with opposite gender friends, developing friends of other cultures, issues of rights and freedoms, and expectations for academic performance.

Further, it is important to appreciate that immigrant families come to America generally seeking to provide a better life for their children than what might have been available in their country of origin. Hence, when these parents come up against conflict with their children owning to adaptation, the conflict can be felt by the parent as tremendous disrespect by the child who doesn't understand the parents' rationale and sacrifice in coming to the new country.

While there are common challenges faced between immigrant parents and children of both gender, risk of pregnancy is a potent issue that can intensify concerns for the well-being of girls. In addition, strong cultural imperatives with regard to dress, deportment and socializing with the opposite sex can at times place greater demands on girls than boys.

These differences can erupt into serious fights between daughters and parents. Even when a fight does not erupt, some teenaged girls may seek to lead a double-life; keeping secrets about relationships and even their dress when at school or in the community. Other teenaged girls may seek to subordinate their feelings to the will of their parents, only to find themselves depressed and anxious over the difficulty with cultural and family adaptation.

Boys do face cultural imperatives and conflicts too, but the absence of risk of pregnancy can lessen the scrutiny placed upon them by parents. However, the boys may be more subject to high expectations for academic excellence, which may or may not be taken well. If not taken well, boys may come to reject their own family's culture, falling prey to the illusions of freedom from authority by gravitating to counter-culture groups or gangs. This in turn can lead to a risk of conflict with the law and abject academic failure as well as extreme conflict with their family.

The challenge is on the parents to adapt and find reasonable strategies to support cultural expectations in view of the greater likelihood that their children will be affected and changed by the new host culture. It is less a question of whether the children will be changed by the host culture, but rather how and to what degree.

Further, some immigrant parents may hail from cultures where the norm is to tell a child what to do and expect obedience. This quickly erodes for the children socialized particularly in western culture where individual freedom is valued and rewarded. Thus, those parents who adjust and develop strategies that minimize the risk of conflict with their children stand the opportunity to remain more influential in their children's lives than those parents who rely solely upon control strategies.

While not nagging their children, sharing stories as to why parents chose to immigrate and their hopes for their family's future can inform their children as to their family aspirations. Further, when parents invite their children to engage in a dialogue about the differences between their respective lives non-judgmentally, parents and children may be apprised of their respective experiences and may be in a better position to discuss differences between themselves.

The challenge here is for the parents to develop skills that rely more upon influence than control. This can also be facilitated by participation and enjoyment of cultural activities and inviting their children's new friends to join in. Co-opting children's friends can serve as a better way of maintaining family integrity than isolating from friends.

(Source: Gary Direnfeld, MSW. SWHELPER 2017)

CHAPTER 4

BE AN INFORMED IMMIGRANT ABOUT U.S. COURT SYSTEM

"Let your intimate friends be chosen from such as are better informed than yourself." - Robert Shumann

Many immigrants are surprised to hear that, "if you plead guilty or are found guilty at the court of law, you can be deported."

Most immigrant are not aware of this fact. Consequently, large numbers of immigrants get deported each year based solely on the outcome of their court cases. This is happening even more so with the current administration.

This is why it's important to have an attorney representing you, especially if it's a serious matter that you are dealing with.

What you don't know will hurt you. You need to be informed about a few things related to court procedures and how to behave in a courtroom.

You must be in court on time.

I did extensive work as a court interpreter at various courts in the U.S. One thing that I observed was that immigrants and members of refugee community are notorious for getting to court late for scheduled hearings.

You must be in court on time. Check your court notice that you got in the mail for the exact time. You should always call the Court Administrator to confirm the exact date and time. If you are late or don't appear, you risk being held in contempt and a warrant being issued for your arrest. If you aren't a U.S. citizen, an order of arrest can jeopardize your ability to become a citizen or achieve legal status.

If you haven't hired an attorney (who in this case might confirm your court date for you), call the Court Administrator at least one day before your scheduled appearance and make sure that you are on the court's calendar. You don't want to travel to court only to learn that you should have called the court first to learn that you case has been rescheduled or something of that nature.

How should I dress for my court appearance?

Your appearance is important. You should dress in your Sunday best. Treat the court matter seriously. I see too many defendants appear in court like they just rolled out of bed. Make sure you are neat and presentable.

The judge and prosecutor have a very short period of time to deal with your case.

What if I am not a U.S. Citizen?

Depending with the seriousness of your case, the judge is supposed to tell you that if you plead guilty or are found guilty, you can be deported. If you leave the U.S. you may not be allowed to re-enter. Also, if you apply for legal status or citizenship in the future, a conviction may cause your request to be denied.

Take this matter seriously. Immigration is covered by Federal Law. Even a seemingly minor violation in one state can have profound implications on your immigration status. Consult with an experienced immigration attorney before your case is decided.

Adopted from: Adres Mejer Law: Notes on Court Etiquette

CHAPTER 5

STAY INFORMED ABOUT IMMIGRATION

"Information and ignorance are like light and darkness . . . When light comes into your room, darkness must fly away. When information rules your mind, ignorance finds its way out!" - Israelmore Ayivor

Misinformation related to immigration abounds in social media and sadly this is where many uninformed immigrants go to look for answers. And so having the right information at all times will keep away incorrect information that results into negative consequences.

A U.S. green card opens many doors of opportunities to immigrants, but not all of them, as some immigrants are made to believe – not until you become a U.S citizen.

Also, some immigrants are not aware that permanent residency is not the same as citizenship, and it isn't always permanent. Minor infractions may result in serious consequences.

Many permanent residents have been deported by immigration officials including those with protected status under DACA, too quickly for anyone to prevent it. It's illegal, but that doesn't mean it doesn't happen.

In my early years in America, I didn't know that permanent residents have to go through separate immigration lines from citizens in many airports, away from family members who are American citizens. I had to experience it myself in order to learn about it.

Also, permanent residents cannot leave the country of their residence for periods longer than six months or less. They are required to check in with immigration officials before doing so to prevent serious problems with their immigration status in the future.

When all is said and done, the United States is the land of opportunity. You will understand it shortly upon arrival if you are new here. Don't ever forget it, and don't waste it. Many people risked their lives to have this chance (opportunities) to realize their personal potential and reach their wildest dreams. I hope you learn to make use of every opportunity that comes your way.

I decided to include this subject in this material because I want to clear misinformation, because misinformation abounds, which eventually causes a lot of mistrust and confusion about which information is correct.

I have found that, the most effective way to fight misinformation is to listen to experts on any given topic. I want to help fight misinformation that you might be exposed to by letting you hear what experts have to say about this subject and many others related to it here below.

Adres Mejer Law Experts and_The American Dream Team have a done a great work in the area of research and sharing what I believe to be important information, ideas and suggestions that I'm about to share with you. They provide information on:

- The different categories of immigration status in the U.S.
- How to become a U.S citizen
- Questions related to dual citizenship
- Life in America
- Which state to make your home
- Understanding where most immigrants live
- How to find a place to live in the USA

Most immigrant are not aware of the Categories of Immigration Status in the U.S. Knowing the number of categories and how people find themselves in each one of them is important because you will understand which one you fall into and how to move between them or move up to the next one when appropriate.

There are four Categories of Immigration Status in the U.S. Since a criminal conviction can complicate your immigration process, the categories of certain crimes are also explained in this article. Applying these concepts can make all the difference in any immigration petition.

To begin with, let's look at the four types of immigration status that exist: citizens, residents, non-immigrants and undocumented. The characteristics of each status are explained below.

U.S. Citizens

These are people who were either born in the U.S. or who have become "naturalized" after three or five years as permanent residents. Citizens can never be deported, unless the citizenship was obtained through fraud. You can work legally and receive any public benefits you qualify for. In addition, you can petition for the legal status of your spouse, child, parent or sibling.

Permanent or Conditional Residents

a) **Legal Permanent Residents (LPRs)** are those who have a "green card." A green card holder, or lawful permanent resident, is someone who has been granted authorization to live and work in the United States on a permanent basis. As proof of that status, you are granted a permanent resident card, commonly called a green card. You can become a permanent resident through a number of different ways. Most individuals are sponsored by a family member or employer in the U.S. Other individuals may become permanent residents through refugee or asylee status or other humanitarian programs. In some cases, such as when your spouse can't or won't file for you, you may be eligible to file for yourself.

b) **Conditional Residents** are those who had been married less than two years before they received their green card. This type of residency requires that you and your spouse jointly file to remove the condition within two years of receiving your green card, or the card will be terminated and you will face deportation.

To convert your conditional status to permanent status, you will need to submit a Petition to Remove the Conditions on Residence (Form I-751), with supporting evidence and the appropriate fees, up to 90 days before your conditional residence status expires. If you apply before the 90-day limit, the application will be returned to you. If you fail to file before the two-year anniversary, your card and your conditional residence status will both expire and you could be deported. You have a three-month window to file your application. You must submit, in a timely manner, the application, the appropriate filing fee and any supporting evidence in order to qualify.

Both types of residents have permission to live and work permanently in the U.S. unless they are guilty of a serious criminal offense or some other immigration violation. If you are a resident, you can also petition for legal status for your spouse or child.

Generally, if you have been a lawful permanent resident for five years, you can apply to become a naturalized U.S. citizen. But if you were granted a green card based on marriage to a U.S. citizen, then you can apply after three years. Just because you received a green card doesn't mean you will automatically become a citizen. You have to show that you deserve it. If at some point you were arrested for any reason, if you owe any taxes or have failed to pay child support, you should discuss your matter with an immigration attorney before filing.

Non-Immigrants

People who fall into this category are in the country legally, but only on a temporary basis. Examples include:

Students (F-1 visa)

Business visitors or tourists (B1/B2 visas)

Fiancées (K-1 visa)

Individuals granted temporary protected status.

In general, recipients of these visas don't intend to immigrate. If the application is fraudulent or you overstay or otherwise violate the terms of the visa, your legal status will change to undocumented. Even so, a high percentage of undocumented immigrants came on legal visas (like my family initially did).

Undocumented

People who are in the country without permission, or illegally, are called undocumented. This means they do not have permission to live in the U.S. They are not authorized to work and they have no access to public benefits like health-care or a driver's license.

Any person who is undocumented runs the risk of being deported or having deportation proceedings started against them at any time. This creates a highly stressful and unstable living situation.

There are two ways people can become undocumented. The first is to overstay a legal temporary visa. The second is to enter the U.S. without going through a port of entry.

Source: Andres Mejer Law

CHAPTER 6

HOW TO BECOME A U.S. CITIZEN

"Patriotism means to stand by the country. It does not mean to stand by the president or any other public official." - Theodore Roosevelt

Many immigrants have little or no access to accurate information concerning immigration. According to a recent survey, most immigrants are "flying blind" when it comes to understanding how to become a U.S. citizen.

Here is helpful information from the experts in this field.

Participating in the Green Card Lottery is the first step to emigrating to the USA. As each day goes by, the USA feels more and more like home and before you know it, you will be applying for a U.S. citizenship! Becoming a U.S. citizen is the ultimate fulfillment of the American dream for many around the world.

Receiving the U.S. citizenship is your way of showing your loyalty and commitment to the United States of America. By accepting, you agree to the responsibilities of being a U.S. citizen and agree to respect the laws of the country and its peoples. A U.S. citizenship gives you the same rights and privileges that all Americans have. A U.S. citizen has more responsibilities than a Green Card holder, but the privileges are worth it.

All U.S. citizens, for example, have the right to vote in all elections and help decide who will become President of the United States. Moreover, citizens can serve on a court jury and apply for federal and state jobs which are only reserved for American citizens. There are no limitations to the amount of time you spend outside of the USA if you are a U.S. citizen. Furthermore, citizens can issue petitions to have family members come to the USA and get a Green Card.

The process of applying for U.S. citizenship is called naturalization. Green Card holders or children of U.S. citizens can apply for American citizenship. Generally, the following requirements must be met to be eligible:

- You must be at least 18 years of age at the time that you apply (Application for Naturalization).
- You must have lived in the USA for at least five years as a permanent resident (Green Card holder) or for 3 years if married to and living with a US citizen.
- You must have lived at least 30 months of the last five years in the USA and 18 months of the last three years if married to and living with a U.S. citizen.
- You have lived in the same U.S. state or USCIS district for at least three months before applying for naturalization.
- You must pass an English and a Civils Test as well as prove your understanding of the U.S. Constitution.
- You must uphold and respect the laws of the United States of America and show what is called good moral character.

If any of the following points apply to you, then it is possible that your application process will be different:

- You, your partner, child or deceased parent served in the U.S. military.
- You are a so-called U.S. National. You or one of your parents were born in an American territory.
- You are applying for right of residency under the Amnesty Law of 1986.
- You are a refugee or asylum seeker.
- You are married to a U.S. citizen who is frequently deployed abroad.
- You lost your U.S. citizenship under an earlier law when you married a non-U.S. citizen.
- You are employed by a recognized American institute or international organization.

Those who successfully apply for a U.S. citizen can be proud to call an American passport their own.

Dual Citizenship

Taking on the US citizenship is very exciting. Understandably, it also raises the question of what will happen to your current citizenship. For example, do you need to give up your citizenship to become an American? According to U.S. law, becoming a U.S. citizen does not mean having to give up your previous citizenship. This means that having dual citizenship in the USA is allowed.

People applying for U.S. citizenship, however, must find out if their home country allows for a second citizenship. Some countries require citizens to meet certain requirements before taking on a second citizenship. It is important to inform yourself of U.S. as well as your home country's requirements so that you may successfully become a dual citizen!

Source: Adopted from The American Dream: About living in the USA

CHAPTER 7

LIVING IN THE US

"Learn everything you can, anytime you can, from anyone you can, there will always come a time when you will be grateful you did." - Sarah Caldwell

Many immigrants pleasantly get to learn that a life in the USA means having a wealth of options.

With a surface area of a little under 10 million square kilometers, the USA is the third largest country in the world. You can make the USA your new home and find your dream job in the U.S. state of your choice. Whether you prefer a bustling metropolis or a quiet town, everybody will find their dream location in the USA.

Perhaps you are asking yourself, which U.S. state should I live in?

As an immigrant in U.S. you are in for a treat when it comes to the choices you have in regard to where to live. When I was new in U.S. this was not clear, but it became clear later on. I didn't realize how spoilt I was for choices about where to live.

Which of the fifty breathtaking U.S. states should you live in?

America is famous for its diversity. If you have already been there – either as a tourist, a student or you reside here now – you know what I am talking about when I say how beautiful and different every corner of the USA is. Climate and people change as you go from the east coast to the west coast. Wherever you go in the USA, you are sure to meet Americans who will proudly tell you their family's immigration story. According to the United States Census Bureau, there were around 43.1 million first-generation (foreign born) people living in the United States in 2015, and they comprised about 13.5% of the U.S. population.

The population of America is just as multi-faceted as its climate, landscapes, flora and fauna. If you prefer the rugged mountains, isolation and an artic climate, then you might prefer Alaska. Those who prefer the sun, beaches and a tropical climate will find everything they want and more in Florida. When you are here, your options are open!

Climate in the USA

The climate in the USA is one of the most popular reasons why so many people dream of living in America. Below is a rough overview:

South

In the South, the climate is more tropical with hot, humid summers and pleasant temperatures in winter. If you want to bathe in the sun all day without the humidity, then Arizona, southern California, New Mexico and Nevada in the southwest might be the perfect place for you.

Northeast

Residents in the Northeast get to experience all four seasons. The U.S. states of Maine, Vermont and New Hampshire are famous for their colorful fall foliage. Winter in the Northeast is often harsh with lots of snow and ice storms.

West

If you prefer high mountains and the alpine climate of the West, then you will feel at home in the Rocky Mountains. In the Rockies, the air is relatively dry and in winter, you should expect heavy snowfall and below-zero temperatures.

Northwest

Washington and Oregon, located in the northwestern corner of the USA, are well-known for being rainy. The charming island-dotted Pacific coast and the Cascade mountains, however, make up for all the rain.

The most popular regions in the USA: where do most immigrants live?

California

When it comes to the total number of immigrants, California is by far the most popular state for immigrants. In 2014, California was home to 10.5 million foreign-born people, making 27% of its population immigrants. The most well-known cities in California are San Francisco, San Diego, and of course Los Angeles. Who doesn't immediately think of Hollywood glam when they think of the city of angels? In recent years, California has also been immediately associated with the IT and high-tech industry in Silicon Valley.

TIP: Despite an 8-laned highway, dealing with traffic is all part of living in Los Angeles. Living close to your work has clear advantages and will save you time on your morning commute. Surprisingly, California also has many ski resorts.

New York

With 4.5 million immigrants, New York state ties Texas for second place. New York City is by far the United States' biggest metropolis. The Big Apple is home to financial institutions, overcrowded streets, exploding housing prices and expensive restaurants and at its center is Manhattan. If you are searching for a little more peace and affordable housing, then you might be more successful in Harlem, Brooklyn or on the other side of the Hudson River in New Jersey. I lived in New Jersey for several years when I initially become a student in America.

Texas

Texas is also home to around 4.5 million immigrants. The cowboy and barbeque-loving state of Texas is the second biggest and the second most populated U.S. state. The Lone Star State is famous for being the only state besides Vermont that was an independent republic before becoming a U.S. state in 1846. Its capital is Austin, although most people are more familiar with Houston. It has the second highest economy in the United States, which is not a surprise because of its diverse economy – which is good for immigrants. A large part of its economy is boosted by oil companies as well as a developing tech-industry.

FLORIDA

The sunny beaches of Florida are home to 4 million immigrants who are living their American dream to the fullest! It is not nicknamed the Sunshine State for nothing: Nowhere else in the USA has as many sunny days as Florida. Its beautiful weather and beaches as well as Everglades National Park attract many tourists a year – and they all want to stay!

The most popular cities are Miami Beach, Fort Lauderdale, South Beach, Tampa and the area around Naples on the west coast. Tourism and agriculture are big factors driving Florida's economy. Did you know that 50% of all citrus fruit comes from the Sunshine State?

Source: Adopted from The American Dream: About living in the USA

CHAPTER 8

HOW DO I FIND A PLACE TO LIVE IN THE USA?

"Who you are tomorrow begins with what you do today." - Tim Fargo

To find a house to live in America is like finding a job, because to get a job you need to be in the country for the interview most of the time.

So, the first step is moving to the USA and the second is deciding where you want to live.

There are a few things you should know before you start searching for a house or apartment in the USA. Firstly, it helps if you already have a job because a sizable percentage of your salary will be used for housing in the USA – unless you are being hosted by someone. But even then, if you have a job, I would suggest you do your best to chip in towards your upkeep.

Many immigrants, members of refugee community including Green Card holders live with family or friends when they first move to the USA. Even though it is possible to search for a house or apartment online (before you leave for the states), it is much easier to get housing when you are already in the USA. Moreover, most landlords want to meet their potential tenants personally, and you too want to see the place where you might be living in. Searching for housing in the USA works best when you are already in the USA.

Important housing terms

As a fresh American resident searching for a house or apartment, you may come up against some unfamiliar words. So that you can concentrate on searching for a house rather than a word in a dictionary, I would like to introduce you to some English words you will come across. Below is a list of important housing terms as well as tips to finding your dream home:

- Keep an eye out for "Apartment Available" or "For Rent" signs on buildings and community boards located in local libraries, grocery stores, community centers, etc.
- Look in local newspapers for a section called the "Classified Ads." Here, you will find a list of homes and apartments for buying or renting in your region.

- If you would like to have someone search for you, look in the yellow pages (phone book) for "Property Management" or "Realtor." These entities will offer their services for free if you are renting from or through them, or for a small price if you are just interested in their service. They will find a home according to your preferences. I have utilized their services few times now, especially when I would move to a new town or state.
- Ask a friend, family or colleague if they know of any available apartments or houses.
- There are many sites on the internet that list housing, but be careful to only visit well-known and trustworthy websites.

Immigrants and members of refugee community have the right to buy or rent property in the USA. There are a few things, however, that you should be aware of. Many landlords require you to show them your Social Security Card before signing the contract. Also, you will need to show proof of your salary (income). Usually, a pay slip will serve this purpose. If you do not yet have a job or the money needed, someone else can vouch for you.

RENTAL CONTRACT

Before you sign any contract otherwise known as a lease, you should make sure that you completely understand all the terms and conditions. For how long will the contract last? If I move out, how early in advance must the landlord know (usually 30 days)? Who is responsible for repairs? Are utilities included in the rental price? Will there be additional costs (water, gas, electricity, trash disposal, etc.)? Take time to go over every word of the contract and, if necessary, have a native speaker help you.

BUYING A HOUSE IN THE USA

For many people, buying a house in the USA is a big step towards fulfilling their American dream. Buying a house is a huge responsibility, but has many advantages. If you are interested in buying a house, you should contact a real estate agent to help you. It is best to ask friends or family if they have recommendations. Many Americans who buy a house take out a loan which is called a "mortgage." Make sure to get financial advice from a bank before making any big purchases.

If you do buy a house, the first thing you should do is buy the appropriate insurance. There are several types of housing insurances, e.g. for weather damage, fire or theft, so make sure you contact a trustworthy insurance salesman to guide you in the process.

Tip: Don't forget to keep USCIS (U.S. Citizenship and Immigration Services) informed of your new address if and when you move.

Source: Adopted from The American Dream: About Living in the USA

CHAPTER 9

FAMOUS IMMIGRANTS IN THE USA

"Give me but a firm spot on which to stand, and I shall move the earth."
– Archimedes

Most immigrants are surprised to hear that many of America's most famous people were immigrants. From scientists, writers and architects, to politicians, athletes and artists. Every one of them started with a dream before they become famous. The USA gives immigrants a place to shine; immigrants are what make America great. The list of famous US immigrants is ever growing. And who knows, you may be next!

Now is your chance to start working on your dream to make it a reality. Some years from now, you will look back at this time as the moment that you started your life-long journey towards your success in America.

The American Dream Team has done a great work of putting together a list of famous immigrants in the USA and shared great points on it in a way that makes reading them enjoyable and insightful.

I would like to give you a taste of two prominent figures in American from that list.

Albert Einstein – Physicist

Everyone recognizes the picture of the man with wild, white hair sticking out his tongue – Albert Einstein.

Albert Einstein is the most famous and prominent physicist of all time. Nobody has influenced their field as much as this immigrant from Germany did. Naturally, every university in the USA wanted to host him as a professor.

Albert Einstein first visited the USA in 1920 after Princeton University convinced him to come and give a lecture on his Theory of Relativity. Between 1930 and 1933, Einstein then traveled back and forth between Germany and California.

During his stay at the California Institute of Technology in Pasadena,

Hitler came to power in Germany. On April 17, 1933, Einstein refused to ever set foot in Germany again, moved to Princeton, New Jersey to work at the Institute for Advanced Studies and thus became a US immigrant. On October 1, 1940, he became a U.S. citizen and lived in Princeton, New Jersey until his death.

Madeleine Albright – U.S. Secretary of State

Even though you must be born in the USA to become a US president, there are still many political positions that are open to people born outside of the USA. Madeleine Albright, who was U.S. Secretary of State under President Bill Clinton from 1997-2001, is a prime example of what immigrants in the USA can achieve.

Madeleine Albright was born in former Czechoslovakia and in 1948 came to the United States with her parents who were fleeing communism. Her parents settled in Denver, Colorado and in 1957, she became a U.S. citizen. She studied political science and received her master's and doctorate degree from Columbia University in New York City. She worked for the National Security Council as well as Georgetown University as a professor. In 2001, she became the first female Secretary of State and a role-model for women and immigrants. Albright is still very active politically and was awarded the Presidential Medal of Freedom in May 2012.

Other influential U.S. immigrants include movie producer Ang Lee, the actor and politician Arnold Schwarzenegger, the actress Charlize Theron, the soccer player Freddy Adu, the baseball player Sammy Sosa, the entrepreneur Liz Claiborne . . . and many others!

As I mentioned earlier, now it's your turn; make your own personal American dream a reality.

Source: Adopted from The American Dream: About Living in the USA

CHAPTER 10

YOUR RIGHTS AS AN IMMIGRANT PATIENT IN THE U.S.

"It is not often that a man can make opportunities for himself. But he can put himself in such shape that when or if the opportunities come he is ready."
- Theodore Roosevelt

Most immigrants are surprised to know that they have a huge list of rights when they show up at a hospital in the U.S. as patients. Yes, you have rights. Whether you are there on outpatient basis, or you are admitted (inpatient), you have equal rights as everyone else. Many immigrants don't know this. This is because in many of their native countries, patients have no rights nor do they get informed about their care while at the hospital. Many are told to undergo tests and procedures that they are not informed about, or they are given treatment that they have not authorized. Even when a patient wants to lodge a complaint for mistreatment, there is no set process for sharing their grievances. In some cases, the patients face threats of unspecified consequences if they lodge a complaint in some of these countries.

When you show up for your appointment or become an inpatient in a U.S. hospital, you will receive a copy of your rights as a patient. In general, most hospitals have the following statement as their guide on how they will provide care for you:

"Your health and safety are important to us. We will do our best to make you as comfortable as possible."

Many hospitals in the U.S. try their best to make your experience wonderful. Many of them even have what they call a **Patient Experience Department**. Part of the role of this department (office) is to receive feedback from the patients about their experience (both positive and negative) during the time they received care. Don't forget to make use of Patient Experience Department if needed to share your experiences during or after a hospital visit or stay.

TIP: Positive patient experience can drive up good-will and patient traffic. This alone is a motivation for many hospitals to provide you with high quality care and services.

Here are the most basic rights that you have as a patient in the U.S.

Use of emergency room.

It might surprise you to know that you have a right to treatment when you visit the hospital emergency room (ER), also known as emergency department.

Emergency room staff are legally required **not** to ask you about payment information before you see a doctor or receive care.

What this basically means is that:

The staff should not attempt to figure out your ability as a patient to pay for care, the reason being that this can be seen as discouraging patients from seeking services at the ER.

Rights to privacy.

You have the following rights:

1. Notice of privacy practice.
   The hospital will give you a written notice of their policies and procedures on protected health information. The hospital will maintain the privacy of your protected information in accordance with State and Federal Law. Only with your written permission will the hospital release your medical information.
2. Inspect and copy.
   You have the right to look over at or get copies of your health records.
3. Change information.
   You have the right to ask the hospital to change your health records if you feel that there is a mistake in what has been entered in them.
4. You have a right to file a complaint with the state or federal government if you believe your rights or your privacy rights have been violated (this includes feeling that you have been discriminated against). In the U.S., hospitals post contact details of where to file a complaint somewhere visible at the hospital in the patient registration or wait area. This information will be shared with you through your interactions with the hospital staff and through their correspondence with you even when it's posted.
   TIP: you will not be penalized for filling a compliant.

5. Request confidential communication.
   You have the right to ask that the hospital or your provider share information with you in a certain manner or at a certain place. For example, you may ask the hospital to send information to an alternative address instead of your home address.

   I suggest you make these types of requests in writing and mail them or drop them at the hospital or the clinic, especially if you are not having a face to face appointment with the provider when you decide to make these changes.
6. List of disclosures
   You have the right to ask for a list of the times when your health information was released and to whom.

Health insurance, co-pay and the cost of your health care

I want to share briefly here below few points about your healthcare payment-out of pocket expenses.

Many people don't know that they can find out how much they will have to pay for their healthcare, including co-payment (out of pocket expenses) before they receive care. I have observed many people struggle with medical debts that they were not prepared for and hence find it difficult to plan or figure out how to pay because they didn't have this information beforehand.

To find out how much your test, treatment, or service will cost you, including how much your health insurance will cover talk to your health-care provider. The specific amount you'll owe may depend on several things, like:

1. How much is allowable by your insurance coverage.
2. How much your doctor charges.
3. Whether your doctor accepts the assignment.
4. The type of facility.
5. Where you get your labs, test, or service done.

Your doctor or other health care provider may recommend you get services more than your insurance covers. Or, they may recommend services that your insurance doesn't cover. If this happens, you may have to pay some or all of the costs. Ask questions so you understand why your doctor is recommending certain services and whether your health insurance will pay for them.

TIP: Your local hospital or the hospital you are being seen has financial assistance you can apply to help pay for your medical bills if you don't have health insurance or it's inadequate to pay for your treatment. Ask to speak with a staff member in financial assistance department of the hospital you are receiving care.

CHAPTER 11

THINGS IMMIGRANTS WISH THEY KNEW EARLY

"I didn't flee a dictator or swim an ocean to be an American like some do. I just thought long and hard about it." - Craig Ferguson

Read through this sampling and see if you are represented. If you find something you wish you knew before, that you know now, and it's not in the list, write to us or share on our website. It might help someone.

Several immigrants have mentioned a variety of topics, like taxes, high price of medical care, and many more, which I share below. But before we get to that, here is a summary of some of the subjects that most immigrants would have wanted to know about before coming to America. This summary might help you to know where to start researching so you can find answers for those topics that are important to you before it's too late.

I wish I knew everything about taxes.

I wish I knew more than just buying health insurance when it comes to healthcare.

I wish I knew about public transportation.

I wish I knew about gun violence.

I wish I knew a lot more about insurance, not just for health, but also, for car, life, renter's and everything else.

I wish I knew about Immigration laws, and the mountain of uncertainty involved in your future stay in this country given the volatile situation we are in right now, and the increasing difficulty involved in getting a work visa or green card.

I wish I knew about application processing times for various visas and the fact that I cannot leave the country while certain visa applications are in process at USCIS.

I wish I knew I could not bring my parents to this country when they retire back home and need my support and care for long life.

Sampling of things

Here is the sampling of things most immigrants wish they knew before they landed in America. For some of them, their views were shaped by their experiences after living in the U.S. for more than twenty to thirty years.

#1. Education is your priority

Don't be afraid to have multiple degrees or trade certificates in different industries. Those papers can come in handy during a recession. You can also use your training in school to make extra income. For example, if you are an automotive technician, you can fix and/or sell cars on the side for profit. A realtor can buy rental properties. A truck driver can start a fleet of trucks. A policeman can moonlight as a security guard and a fireman can do inspection and maintenance of fire sprinklers systems part-time.

#2. That I may not get to know my neighbors

Growing up in a country where everybody knows and is informed about everyone else, this was very hard to fathom. In India, I not only knew my neighbors but we were all very bonded.

We exchanged food very often. I got to try so many dishes from different cultural backgrounds!

When my mom had to leave town for a few days, the moms in the neighborhood got me food - every single day.

I played games and spent relaxing evenings with my neighbors, sometimes at their house, sometimes at mine.

We watched movies together.

But here in U.S., I've tried to chat my neighbors up but their demeanor tells me they are not interested and/or do not have the time to make a conversation. I ended up finally asking a colleague that I am friends with, "How do you get to know your neighbors around here?" His response was, "Ahaha. You don't!"

I've lived in the same apartment for over a year and I still do not know my neighbors. But, I am stubborn. So, I intend to continue trying.

#3. Your salary per year is not what you actually get paid

Income taxes. Your salary per year is not what you actually get paid. If you work for an employer, a big chunk of your salary is being taken for federal taxes, state taxes (with exception of few states), and depending on where you live, city and/or county taxes. The higher your salary is, the more is being taken out. When we lived in New York City, almost 35% of our salary was paid in taxes. So, your $10000 a year is actually around $70000 there. If you run your own business, you'd still have to pay about as much, come the tax season in April of each year. The first time I filed taxes, my heart dropped. I actually owed a bit more to the government than what was deducted from my already miserable salary because I didn't know what deductions were and how the heck to claim them. Thinking of not paying taxes to Uncle Sam? Like Jerry Seinfeld said, the government can come and take anything they want from you, they are like the mafia.

#4. Without health insurance, healthcare is restrictively expensive

Cost of healthcare. If you've been enjoying a free or cheap healthcare in your home country, forget about it here unless you're poor (which is not fun). You have to get your health insurance through an employer, private insurance company, or since 2014, through Affordable Health Care Act (which only sounds affordable but is actually not, unless, again, you're poor). Monthly premiums for health insurance vary dramatically from employer to employer, from company to company and from income to income. It can be as "little" as $400 a month for a family to as much as $2500.

Just remember, having a good health insurance coverage helps. This is why: if you don't have one, you might end up selling your entire assets just to clear up your medical bill.

#5. Hollywood lies

Well, this is something any foreigner will tell you; you know how in movies, beautiful people are shown driving new cars, living in beautiful homes, working in beautiful offices, etc? This is not how an average American person looks and lives like. Just put on some local news and see the real everyday USA. You'd probably think much better of your home country. I'm not kidding.

#6. Language

You might think you know English pretty well before you immigrate to the U.S., but once you are here, you will invariably encounter some slang and expressions you are not familiar with – especially if, like most foreigners, you studied British English at home. A lot of common American English expressions come from baseball, football, and some movies and shows you have not seen or even heard about.

Speaking of the language – you will probably find out that the hardest thing is to understand people when they are talking to each other and not directly to you. This is because when talking to you, people will want to be understood and thus they will, consciously or unconsciously, adjust their speech accordingly.

You will, more likely than not, be less articulate here than you were at home, and this can last for years if not decades. If you came here after age sixteen or so, your accent will probably stay with you for a long time, most likely forever.

#7. Humor

You might find that American humor does not seem especially funny to you; worse, your own attempts to be humorous might not go well until your American English is nearly perfect and you have lived here for a while. Be careful with jokes ridiculing someone's race, gender, sexual orientation or their weight – these will definitely not be taken well.

#8 Shared experiences

It might seem to you that at first you don't have anything in common with people who grew up here or have lived here for a very long time – they celebrate different holidays (Thanksgiving, Independence Day, Labor Day, etc.), watch different sports (football and baseball are not watched in most other countries), their high school and college experience was probably very different from yours, etc. Many Americans, especially those who are not college-educated and/or well-traveled, will not speak your language (or any other foreign language for that matter), will know next to nothing about your culture (and maybe hold a few stereotypes about it), will not be able to relate to you and your experiences, and sometimes will find your ways of doing things weird or unusual. (This is not because they are close-minded or xenophobic, although this certainly can be the case; more often, it is because the education system here is generally not doing a sufficiently good job teaching about other countries and cultures). This is especially true if you are not in a major metropolitan area where there is a lot of diversity. Thus, you might feel like you are a stranger in a strange land. Luckily, after a few years here, these feelings will disappear or at least will not be as strong. And eventually you will feel that you have more in common with people here than with people in your birth country.

#9. Education

If you are well-educated, you might find that a few people you will deal with here are not familiar with some facts you consider basic. Occasionally some folks will make comments or ask you questions about your country that you might consider a bit awkward or downright stupid (for example, they might assume that just because you come from a poorer country and speak English with an accent, you are poor and uneducated and so they talk to you in a condescending way). Again, this has more to do with the education system in this country than with people's malice.

Also, the fact is that many well-educated Americans tend to live in neighborhoods and hang out in social circles quite different from where most fresh off the boat immigrants find themselves in at first.

#10. Social circle

Because of the above, you might, especially at first, find yourself surrounded mostly by people from your own culture, including those with whom you probably would never be friends back at home because, other than shared language and culture, they don't have that much in common with you. But, remember that as tempting as it is to stay within your comfort zone where everyone speaks your language and understands your culture, it will definitely pay off to reach out to people outside of your own cultural group. It also goes without saying that, if you are relatively young when you immigrate in the U.S., you will probably wind up having friends from many different countries, not just from your own country.

#11. Cities

American cities are quite different from European and other foreign cities. Public transportation is often limited or nonexistent (exceptions are NYC, Chicago, Boston, and San Francisco); people mostly rely on their cars or use Uber-like services. Cities are sprawled around and, outside of downtowns, have low-rise buildings similar to the ones you find in the suburbs. Some cities and most suburbs are not very walkable; but for those who enjoy walking, there are trails available in parks and other recreation areas.

#12. Food

Due to the diverse population, in many cities and towns you can find excellent restaurants of nearly every possible cuisine. I hadn't tried many of my favorite cuisines before I moved to the U.S. (and, having moved here in my late teens, I did not have much experience dining out anyway).

In many restaurants, portions can be humongous – sometimes two or three times larger than in other countries. However, this is not the case with upscale restaurants; you will find portion sizes there to be much smaller. So, the more expensive the food, the smaller the portion size.

Two things that make dining in the U.S. different from what is common abroad. First, you might feel rushed through your meal. The server will probably frequently check on you asking whether everything is going well and, when they see you are done with your meal, leave a check (bill) "for your convenience" – which is a subtle hint that they want you to vacate the table for the next customer. Second, you are expected to leave at least 15% (preferably 18%-20%) tips. Failure to do so sometimes might be considered rude in some places, even if the service was crappy.

#13. Owning a car

In America it seems you need a car for everything, starting from buying grocery, to going to a hospital. The United States is the 3rd largest nation in the world and has a total land area of 9.834 million square kilometers, which is likely three times the land area of India, a country with the world's second most population with 1.3 billion people living in it.

#14. Imperial system

If you're coming here for your education, then kindly be aware that the U.S uses imperial system. Take time to know the conversions from metric to imperial and vice versa. Being an engineering guy from a country that uses metric system gave me trouble during my early days with the conversion. I remember not knowing what one foot was in inches. Those were my embarrassing days.

#15. Independent life

You might find yourself starting to google stuff like, "*what's loneliness?*" "*what does being lonely feel like?*" I've seen numerous people having a hard time living alone without family.

NOTE: I address how to deal with loneliness in the beginning of this book briefly and again towards the end of the book where I give practical suggestions on things you can do to lessen loneliness while in US.

#16. Having connections

This is very important! Having a person who has lived here for a while is really a great plus. There are close to fifty questions that you may want answered before you land here.

Also, as you interact with other people at work, school, church or other centers of interactions, know that these interactions are vital. Some of them can turn out to be just what you need to find the new apartment you want, or that new job you are looking for. Most of your important recommendation and references that you might need later will come from individuals and entities that you will interact with while here in America.

#17. Routine Life

Your life would be the same as most people here, which is a routine 8 am – 4:30 pm job. Don't get influenced by what you see in movies/TV series.

See Below-Other Things Immigrants Have Suggested as Important to Comprehend

If you have a concern that is not included in this sampling list, please let us know by sharing on our website or sending us an email. We have many immigrants who visit our website and what you share might help someone else.

Majority of immigrants offering these suggestions moved to the U.S. more than twenty-five years ago, before the internet/google era, when many things were very different. Others are not immigrants per se; they are daughters and sons of immigrant parents, but they hear these issues being talked about all the time.

#1. Don't mistake American friendliness for wanting to be friends

We alluded to this earlier.

This one burned me pretty badly when I first came here. *Hey, how are you doing?* It's just a polite form of hello. People don't want to know about your life. Even if the sky has fallen on you, the answer should be "*fine,*" or "*good.*" Any answer other than that will be met with a frown.

Being friendly is a big part of the culture here. It has absolutely nothing to do with wanting to be friends with you. In fact, Americans can be quite slow when it comes to opening up.

#2. Be aware, there are many racists everywhere, who don't need skin color or obvious nationality to hate every immigrant.

Most of the haters alluded to hate all Latin Americans, Caribbean Islanders, Africans and Muslims. Of course, some of them also hate all Irish, Italians, English, French, Germans, Dutch, Belgians, Scandinavians, and especially all Asians. They not only hate people, they also hate schools, any authority and paying bills.

Learn which citizens can be trusted and ask them for guidance.

#3. Do not, under any circumstances, reach out and touch other people's kids

However adorable, friendly and smiley the kids are, unless you have been given explicit permission to touch them by the adult with them, do not do so. Suffice to say that there is a lot of paranoia about sexual predators, however smiley and friendly and well-meaning you are.

Goes for adults, too. No touching beyond a hand shake – never mind your gender and the gender of the other person.

Source: Quora.com (What do you wish you'd known before immigrating to the United States?)

CHAPTER 12

PREVENTION IS BETTER THAN CURE

"Intellectual solve problems, geniuses prevent them." – Albert Einstein

Visionary leaders working for the well-being of their communities creates plans that prevent and mitigate known challenges that individuals and families would face beforehand.

Those plans involve establishing capacity and resources among others to supports members of their communities (I share about them in the next chapter), which can save families and individuals from social and economic catastrophes. Unfortunately, many people (don't be one of them) wait until they are in the worst condition of life before they start looking for help or taking advantage of these resources.

While we are on the subject of "saving families and individuals," I must emphasize that family members, friends and everyone else need to cultivate the culture of looking out for one another. Some people travel thousands of miles to bury a member of their family or a friend, but they couldn't even cross a street to support them when they were alive and in need. Perhaps their help would have prevented the death of their family member, or would have averted the exorbitant bills the family has to worry about now if the problem was addressed when it was still small.

Now, ask yourself this question; am I this kind of a family member? We can also add our friends here and change the question, to ask it this way; am I that kind of a friend?

If you are that kind of a family member or friend, you might want to think of ways you can change that. Find ways you can get involved in improving the lives of those you care about when they are still alive, when they need your help, rather than wait until you hear that they have passed on, then you start the journey to go and bury them.

Two ways to impact positive well-being of individuals and communities alike:

Individual-level interventions

When you make use of available resources and supports, you have the potential of succeeding, or as I like telling my students: at least you have a chance of success, compared to someone who is not making use of what is readily available and accessible to them.

Community-level interventions

Policy makers have the power to address the social and economic conditions that affect community well-being if they so desire to do so. Just the other day, I read an article that reported that in Kansas City, Missouri voters recently approved a ballot initiative that will empower health inspectors to respond to tenant complaints about a broad range of housing conditions, funded by an annual fee of $20 per unit for landlords. Earlier this year, the City Council of Alexandria, Virginia voted to raise the city's meal tax to fund affordable housing. Leaders in these communities and others like them have embraced the need for policy intervention to improve the social needs of their communities and hence impact the well-being of their citizens.

The impact of conditions of our environment on our well-being

The condition of places where people grow up and live have great impact on their well-being in life in general. We know that poverty limits access to healthy foods and forces people to live in unstable housing and unsafe neighborhoods. It also leads to many people receiving sub-standard education.

We also know that more education is a predictor of better outcome on people's well-being.

How does a community impact success of its members? What is the relationship between success of community members and the quality of life their community supports?

I believe that, if many of the barriers found in your communities are removed or reduced, many people living in those communities will start reaching and attaining many of their personal and wellness goals.

The success of many community members hinges on addressing many of the challenges impacting their life right now in the communities where they live. Many of their economical and health challenges could be tackled by addressing the challenges their communities are currently struggling with.

Examples: roads and transportation, affordable housing, accessible clean water, sufficient nutritional food, safe environment, having enough space for walking or bike riding, and issues related to discrimination and prejudice among others.

When individuals' and families' social needs are unmet, there is a direct impact not only on those families but also on the communities they live in. If people are not thriving, it means that they don't have the capacity to help their communities thrive.

How does this affect your health?

As awareness of community effects on its members continues to grow, some researchers have asked whether the effects on health are due to the characteristics of the people who live in the neighborhood rather than the neighborhood itself. This is a question that has not yet been fully answered. Several studies have found, however, that community effects on health continue to hold even after individual characteristics are taken into consideration. For example, one study of residents of different communities whose socio-economic profiles were similar found that individuals in more disadvantaged neighborhoods were more likely to develop heart disease than those living in more advantaged communities.

CHAPTER 13

KNOW WHERE THE RESOURCES ARE IN YOUR COMMUNITY

"Learning is a matter of gathering knowledge; wisdom is applying that knowledge." – Roopleen

In this chapter, I will guide you on what you can do to acquire knowledge of available resources in your community. I'm also interested in encouraging you to go beyond knowledge into action (utilizing this knowledge).

Knowledge is power, I often say (knowing where your resources and supports are), but knowledge by itself is nothing.

We all know there is a big difference between knowing something and doing something (taking action.)

I often tell my students that having knowledge is like having a dream. If you know something about dreams, then you know dreams don't become a reality by themselves. You have to pursue them to achieve them.

So, what do you need beyond knowledge or what I often call power?

You need what I call **active power.** Your power (knowledge) becomes **active** when you make use of it. So, here's how to have active power; go beyond gathering knowledge (learning how to access and use resources, supports and services available in your community) to actually accessing them. This is the only way you will be different from everyone else who also knows about the availability of the resources that you know about. This is the only way these resources will mean something to you, to your family, and to your community.

Remember, when you thrive, you will be at a vantage position to help your community thrive. And so, your community (which is part of those who made these resources and supports available) will eventually benefit by your use of them. This is the ultimate goal of these resources – to benefit everyone.

Most of the supports, resources and services are provided through your **community agencies.**

How do you find the location of community agencies in your area?

Check online or contact your county social services department for resources directory (listing of agencies and providers) found in your community.

This listing will have many of the services and resources listed below as a sample, and many more under community organizations.

The list I offer here is not exhaustive, and your community might have different resources and services available with varying eligibility criteria.

COMMUNITY ORGANIZATIONS

Free Tax Preparation Services

Child and dependent adult abuse Prevention Services

Child Care Services through DHS or community organizations

Clothing, furniture, bus tickets and food donation centers

Crisis Services

Free Medical, dental and eye clinic or funding

Disability Services

Employment and Education support Services

Family & Youth Services

Financial Assistance through DHS or community organizations

Food Assistance through DHS

Health & Dental Services through DHS

Housing through local housing authority or community organizations

Immigrant & Refugee Services

Legal Assistance through local legal aid or pro bono services

Mental Health & Substance Abuse services

Older Adults services

Transportation services

Veterans Services

Energy, heat and water bills funding center

English as Second Language (ESL) programs

Legal Aid services

Basic Needs Programs

These programs offer free resources & services to its residents who are eligible. Many of these programs are run by your county including supports like crisis center and food bank. Many others are run by non-profit organizations in your community.

Examples of these programs or resources/services are:

Food Bank/food pantries

Food pantries supplement groceries to be prepared at home.

Each community has a variety of food bank/pantries. They are run through local government as I mentioned earlier, others are run by local churches and non-profit organizations. I recommend calling the agency to confirm their schedule before going.

Housing and Utility Assistance

They can provide financial assistance for housing and utilities for things like past-due rent, water and energy bills if you meet income eligibility. They do not provide funding though for things like phone bills, cable bills or vehicle repairs, etc.

They can help with:

Bus Tickets

Clothing and Household Items

Box Fans especially during summer

Birth Certificates and Identification documents: funds to order them

Eye Exam and Glasses Assistance

Birthday Bags for Children

Prescription Medication Assistance

Temporary Mailing Address

New Employment Work Items

The Basic Needs Program can help if you have an offer of employment contingent on providing your own boots, non-slip shoes, specific uniform items, etc., and are unable to purchase the items yourself. They require you to bring a dated letter from your employer stating that the items are required to begin working.

Eye Exam and Glasses Assistance

If you have insurance, contact your provider (eye doctor) about receiving an eye exam. If you have a current glasses prescription (after your exam) and are unable to pay for the flames, basic needs program in your community might be able to provide financial assistance to purchase your eyeglasses.

If these two options do not fit your situation: The Basic Needs Program also has a referral program to fund eye exams and glasses with the local providers. Contact them during regular operating hours and ask about assistance with getting eye-exam and eyeglasses.

Prescription Medication Assistance

You can get assistance to refill your prescription through your local free Medical Clinic pharmacy (every community has a free medical clinic) if you don't have insurance. Basic Needs Program can also assist with funding (remember these are run by county government in your city or non-profit organizations).

Local government Run Programs and Others

To access financial support and more, some of these programs require you to prove that you live in that community.

Eligibility

One way to be found eligible apart from income eligibility is proof that you live in that county by showing something with your address, or the address of where you reside in that community. Applicants usually participate in a brief scheduled in-person or phone interview to provide basic information about your household and sign a release form.

When you go to apply for financial assistance (rent or utilities), or for the interview, bring with you a copy of your lease or lender agreement and past due notice/statement if you are applying for housing assistance. When applying for utility assistance, bring the past due statement.

CHAPTER 14

ACCESSING COMMUNITY RESOURCES

"Knowledge counts but common-sense matters." – Louanna Johnson

Am I Eligible?

Each social service center (DHS) has a chart (a guide) that helps you know what programs may be available for you and your family. You can find this chart by contacting your county social services office or visit their website.

For example, there are different criteria for eligibility of services for:

People with Children

People without Children

Legal Immigrants

Undocumented Immigrants

Homeless Individuals and Families

Senior Citizens

Veteran services (many immigrants are also in U.S. military)

What am I Eligible for?

SNAP/ FOOD STAMPS

SNAP benefits, the new name for food stamps, can help put healthy food on the table by providing monthly assistance to purchase food at authorized grocery stores. Benefits are provided monthly through a plastic benefit card, similar to a debit or credit card.

Terms:

EBT

Stands for Electronic Benefit Transfer. It's the system the government uses to disburse benefits.

SNAP

Stands for Supplemental Nutrition Assistance Program. "SNAP benefits" is the same thing as "food stamps."

What should I know?

Employment may not interfere with getting SNAP. Even if you are working, but earning low wages, you may be eligible.

Average SNAP benefits are over $100 per person per month, and $250 or more for families (your state might have different calculations). That means that SNAP benefits for the average family receiving them totals more than $3,000 worth of food support each year.

SNAP Eligibility is based on household size, income, expenses and other factors. Households have to meet income tests to receive benefits, but households that have members who are disabled or elderly (sixty or older) or have out-of-pocket expenses for child care or dependent care, can have higher incomes and still be eligible.

If you meet the income qualifications, it doesn't matter how much money you may or may not have in countable resources. In other words, you can save money for education, a home purchase, or retirement and still receive SNAP benefits.

Other Assistance

There are many organizations that can assist you with matters other than food support, cash assistance and health care coverage that DHS offers. For additional information, call your local department of human services or visit their website for a more complete directory of resources.

Farmers Market

In my state, we have what we call farmers markets that allow customers to buy fresh produce and other homemade products directly from local growers and producers.

You can use SNAP benefits to purchase fresh produce.

Many of these farmers' markets accept EBT/SNAP (food stamps) through what they call the Double Up Food Bucks program, up to $10 spent per market with your SNAP EBT card will be matched when you purchase items from farmers markets.

For a complete list of farmers' markets or to see if your state has one that accepts SNAP benefit, contact your local County Social Services center or visit their website.

Immigrant Eligibility for SNAP

Legal immigrants can receive SNAP benefits if they:

— have lived in the country for five years or more; or

— are children (age eighteen or under).

Ineligible immigrant parents can still receive benefits for their children even if a parent does not qualify.

Certain non-citizens, such as those admitted for humanitarian reasons (refugees), may also be able to receive benefits.

Check with your county social services center to see if your immigration status is negatively affected if you apply for or receive SNAP benefits.

How to Apply for SNAP

You can apply online by vising your county services center website or you can call your state Food Bank Association's Food Assistance Hotline and speak with someone who can help you with the SNAP application (hours are 8:00-4:30 Monday-Friday). You can also apply in-person at your local Department of Human Services office. Call them or check their website to find their physical address and to see if you need an appointment before you go to apply. You don't usually require having an appointment to access services in many of these centers but it's always good to call first if you are able to do so.

Senior Meals

Meals – wheels program

If you are homebound and over the age of sixty, you can receive home-delivered meals up to six days a week or more depending on your county guidelines. Household income does not affect eligibility.

How to Apply

To request Meals-on-Wheels, call Elder Services dept. in your community.

Hot Meal Sites in Your Community

Hot meal sites provide prepared meals during their listed serving times.

I recommend calling the agency to confirm their schedule. Most of these agencies do not require ID or proof of address for you to receive a meal.

Food for Kids

WIC is The Special Supplemental Nutrition Program for Women, Infants, and Children. WIC provides nutritious food and baby formula, health screenings, education, and breastfeeding support. Food is accessed at a store using a benefit card issued by your local WIC program center.

QUICK FACTS

WIC is for low-income pregnant women, breastfeeding and postpartum women, and children up to the age of five.

You can work and still get WIC though there are eligibility guidelines based on family size and gross income.

You can continue to get cash assistance (financial assistance for those who are eligible and qualify) or SNAP benefits food stamps while receiving WIC.

Immigrant eligibility: in many communities all across America, you can get WIC even if you are undocumented or not a citizen especially if your children were born here.

Always check with county social services center to see if your immigration status is negatively affected if you apply for any of these and many other benefits.

How to Apply for WIC

Call your County Social Services office WIC Clinic to schedule an appointment. Be sure to bring the following items to your appointment:

- proof of income or state sponsored health insurance card
- proof of your address
- proof of identity for each family member applying for WIC

Schools and Summer Meals Program

QUICK FACTS

Youth may be eligible for free breakfast before school during the school year. Check your local school for eligibility criteria.

Many public-school students are also eligible for free or reduced-price lunch during school year. An application may be required. Eligibility for school meals for your children is not impacted by immigration status and to my knowledge it does not affect your immigration status either.

In some communities, lunch and breakfast are served for free to all children under nineteen in June, July and August, at many public schools, houses of worship, recreation centers, and community centers. No application or registration is required.

Many of these programs also have backpack give-way events that are offered at some schools or through local community organizations. Many local nonprofit groups and religious organizations hold similar events in service to members of their community right before schools reopens after summer.

Contact your kid's school's social worker also known as student Family Advocate (SFA) in some schools for more information about school breakfast and lunch programs, and to see if your school offers a backpack program.

TIP: SFA might also help you with enrolling your children in your new local school when you relocate to a new community.

Beware

What you need to know about information you give in regard to county, states and federal-run programs when you apply for assistance:

Your Privacy Rights

Even when your information is kept confidential – Federal and State Law limits who can see the information you give them – as part of their work, some of your information might be shared with other agencies. This sharing is part of making sure the information shared with them is complete and correct.

These offices, especially Department of Human Services, might not deny you the services and benefit you apply for and cannot discriminate against you when you apply, but they might share your information with Citizenship and Immigration Service when you utilize some of their benefits as part of their processes to verify your immigration lawful status. But they will not purposely report you to the Citizenship and Immigration Service to let them know that you are in the country illegally if that is the case.

They may however report you to the Citizenship and Immigration Service if you apply for other help, such as Family Investment Program (FIP) and Food Assistance or state Supplementary Assistance. They will not contact the Citizenship and Immigration Service about the people you don't apply for.

Always check with your local DHS center to know which of the information you give them is shared with other agencies, and which agencies are those.

School District Resources

These includes:

Busing your children to and from your home to school.

Free lunch (offered free or at a low price depending with your income) as mentioned earlier.

Medical services for your children through school-based clinics. Schools have full time school nurses available to take vitals and care for children if they fall ill while at school. School-based clinics also have referral processes to outside hospitals and specialty clinics that your children might qualify and be referred for.

There are special needs program for the child and family in need. Counseling and social work services are offered without charge for students within school or through local providers.

Before and after school programs including summer, school arranged programs

After School Programs are provided to your child through your school district

These programs take place at your child's local school or they are facilitated by a separate agency in your community but are run at the school building most of the time. The programs offer children a great start and finish every day, with healthy breakfasts and snacks, plus fun, and educational activities. There are funds available (depending on your income level), to allow your child to attend. You can pick an application or get one mailed to you when you call your school's After Care Program.

After school programs provide children with an opportunity to continue the learning process after the normal hours of school. These programs also allow parents who work to have a safe place to leave their child before and after school. They also offer programing during school break and summer periods, which can be an added support to the kids of newly arrived immigrants and refugee families who might need extra help with their education.

Afterschool

Provide safe and constructive programming that supports children's well-being and school success. Includes after the school day, before school, school break, and summer programs.

Local Library

In America, access to the local library is free. All you need is a library card which is also free.

Your local library is a hub of connection to many things that you can do for free.

First of all, use of a computer and accessing internet is free at your local library. This alone is a big avenue to many of the things you can do by spending quality time at your local library either for educational purposes, searching for relevant and helpful information or doing your homework.

Here is a sample of things you can do at your local library

Check out a variety of books, or read at the library (this is obvious).

Check out variety of movies, cds and documentaries to watch at home with the whole family

As I mentioned earlier, you can use the library space to do your homework and school projects (you can do this alone or as a group).

You can also use the library space for free to hold other important meetings or non-profit activities.

Other things you can do while at the library:

Networking with others to find relevant information online.

Search and apply for employment.

Apply for colleges and other education institutions.

Apply for benefits, scholarship and other related items.

Search and apply for housing.

Search for contacts or apply for day care services.

The libraries carry a lot of books for your kids to check out. They also have computers set aside for kids loaded with games that children can play.

Sample of Resources Provided at Your Local Libraries

Free tax preparation.

Many libraries have this resource or have a list of where to find help with tax preparation.

English as a Second Language – ESL

Many libraries offer free ESL classes or provide a list of where these classes are offered in your community.

Almost all local libraries hold citizenship test preparation programs or can help you with access to these materials.

Library Resource Center

Most libraries now have a separate area where you can find a list of the many resources available in your community in addition to the following services.

A rider's guide and local bus schedules.

Access to a phone to make free local calls.

Many local libraries are now offering **photocopying** services for a fraction of what you might pay somewhere else and free **faxing** and **scanning** services.

Access to a Network of Regional Universities

Some local libraries now have access to many universities libraries that allow students and locals to have access to these huge reservoirs of material and books. As a student you can even request books and reading materials from these network of universities to be accessed through your local library network.

TIP: libraries are a hub for community members to meet, study, and access research materials.

CHAPTER 15

IMMIGRANT & REFUGEE EMOTIONAL SUPPORTS

"Change doesn't happen by itself. Change requires action." – **Joe Mungai**

In this chapter I will start by addressing emotional challenges that both immigrants and refugee families encounter and suggest ways you can get help. But If you are in a refugee status, I share with you more sources of help that are specifically tailored for you towards the end of this chapter. So, stay tuned. These are support, services and resources that are available right in your home town.

Let's dive in together.

Counseling services are available for free or at a nominal fee, at some select programs run by local churches and non-profit organizations in the community.

These programs offer emotional, mental and health support to immigrants and refugee families. They provide culturally and linguistically appropriate professional services to meet the social and emotional health needs of refugee and immigrants' families.

We all know that immigrants and refugee families must overcome numerous challenges in their homeland during their immigration process and when they are settling here in America. They need to adjust to a culturally, spiritually and socially different life in the United States while they deal with the trauma of their past experiences. Many also need to negotiate the challenges of loss of their homeland identity and the loss of friends and family at the same time during the process of integration.

We also know that, there is scarcity of resources and supports that target immigrants and many refugee families' ongoing psycho-social problems while in America.

I do my share of working with immigrants and refugee families to tackle their psycho-social needs and environment concerns through Center for Families Services Network, a non-profit whose mission is to serve immigrants and members of refugee community (www.center4familyservices.com) I also handle many referrals for many individuals and families who are struggling with trauma and need extra support. As much as I appreciate the opportunity to serve my community, I would quickly add that many more families suffer in silence during their integration period because they lack the knowledge of where to find the little help that is available for them. Either because they don't have contact with others, or they don't know where to start to ask for help.

I encourage you to search for these kinds of services and tap into them or at least know where they are because you might need them once in a while even after settling down in America.

Remember, change doesn't happen by itself. Change requires action.

Select Services Specific to Refugee Population

"Migrants and refugees are not pawns on the chessboard of humanity. They are children, women and men who leave or who are forced to leave their homes for various reasons, who share a legitimate desire for knowing and having, but above all for being more." – **Pope Francis**

Refugee Services Through the Department of Human Services

The Bureau of Refugee Services through collaboration and coordination with your local Department of Human Service empowers refugees to meet their goals as they enrich their hosting state.

These services are available to refugees who have been in the United States for less than 60 months.

Since 1975, the Bureau of Refugee Services has been working with the U.S. Department of State to assist refugees from other countries escape persecution and resettle in the United States. Through a wide array of services, they are able to help refugees and communities adapt to the challenges they are facing while integrating in America.

The Bureau provides a variety of employment related services to refugees that are designed to enable refugees to obtain employment and to improve their employability or work skills.

To learn what services are available to refugees in your home town contact your local Department of Human Services office.

Refugee Vaccination Assistance

Your local Public Health Department might have free services for you or might offer payment options and assistance if you have a refugee status to cover for your vaccinations.

To find the services you can receive from them, call or visit them online to make an appointment. You can also visit them at their office.

Appointments are available for you to complete the I-693 for your one-year health assessment.

Appointments are also available for you and your family to get the vaccines that you need for work, school, and immigration.

Interpreter services are available.

Documents that Might be Needed to Receive Services

For each family member you will need:

Alien number.

(A – number, or USCIS #).

Employment card/Authorization permit or another photo ID.

Previous medical records (if any).

Insurance cards (if any).

If you do not have refugee status and need to find a civil surgeon (certified immigration doctor) to do an immigration physical, visit your local public health department website to find this information.

CHAPTER 16

SERVICES AND SUPPORTS SPECIFIC TO VETERANS AND MILITARY

"We are dealing with veterans, not procedures; with their problems, not ours."
– Omar N. Bradley

I discovered, in the course of my work with members of U.S military and veterans that many veterans from the immigrant community who served in the U.S. military and were discharged honorably lacked knowledge of the resources I share in this chapter.

Allow me to make few observations before I dive right into sharing with you these important resources.

Military culture is often not well understood by the civilian population. Members of military personnel undergo experiences that cannot be understood by those who have not personally experienced it for themselves.

One of the things I learned when working at the department of veteran's affairs as a mental health provider, protecting and defending the interests of the USA are not the only things required of those who serve in the military. With courage and dignity, in times of war, these men and women put their health (physical, emotional and mental), and their lives on the line, for their country.

I also learned that while some may come home to a hero's welcome, others find themselves alienated from their families and communities upon return from many months, sometimes years of duty, in combat regions.

Certainly, all who return from service during times of war return forever changed. Many suffer from physical injuries and almost all suffer from the emotional effects of war that are not visible to us.

My work with them involved helping them navigate the many complicated systems within the federal government, state and various county jurisdictions many came from so as to access their benefits and services. While working with them, I realized that even though there are limited resources to help deal with the many challenges veterans face when they get back home, many of them lacked the knowledge of what is available and where to find it.

Commission of Veteran Affairs

Now, I want to share with you one source (there are many others) that veterans can get support and services from in their county of residence. Every county has what is called Commission of Veteran Affairs that is run according to each state guidelines.

As I share this information with you, I also want you to know this: to find out about other sources of support that are available for you as a veteran that I don't address in this chapter, reach out to your county's Commission of Veteran Affairs Center for guidance in this area. You can search for their contacts on your Social Services Department website or do a quick search online.

Purpose of the Commission

The purpose of the Commission is to assist its county residents who served in the armed forces of the United States and their relatives, beneficiaries, and dependents in receiving from the United States government and the state any and all compensation, pensions, hospitalization, insurance, education, employment pay and gratuities, loan guarantees, or any other aid or benefit to which they may be entitled under any law.

Meaning of Important Terms Relevant to Military Community

- Disability compensation is a monetary benefit paid to veterans who are disabled by an injury or illness while on active duty or by a presumptive condition.
- Pension is a benefit paid to wartime veterans who have limited or no income and who are aged 65 or older, or, if under 65, who are permanently and totally disabled.
- In addition to the Compensation & Pension programs, veterans may be eligible for education and training benefits, a home loan guarantee, life insurance, burial and memorial benefit among other unique services.

Here are additional supports available for the veterans through this office:

Emergency Assistance

This is temporally aid to indigent veterans which can include:

- Paying for utilities and groceries
- Housing financial assistance including finding a place to stay or shelter if you are homeless
- Medical and dental expenses for veterans who are not eligible for Veteran Affairs medical benefits.

Reach out to your local Commission of Veteran Affairs office and see what is available for you.

Tip: This information isn't simply for the purpose of sharing with you what is available to you as an immigrant veteran, or one who is serving in the military; it's also for the purpose of letting you know how and why you should use it to your advantage.

CHAPTER 17

YOUR CHILD HAS FULL RIGHT TO ACCESS LOCAL SCHOOL DISTRICT EDUCATION

"And if we want to achieve our goal, then let us empower ourselves with the weapon of knowledge and let us shield ourselves with unity and togetherness."
– Malala Yousafzai

All children in the United States are entitled to equal access to a basic public elementary and secondary education regardless of their actual or perceived race, color, national origin, citizenship, immigration status, or the status of their parents or guardians.

School districts that either prohibit, discourage, or maintain policies that have the effect of prohibiting or discouraging children from enrolling in schools because they or their parents and guardians are not U.S. citizens or are undocumented may be in violation of Federal Law.

Your school district might have some policies in place that are standard to everyone such as: asking for some documents that can help facilitate enrollment of your kids to their new school.

Below are some examples of acceptable enrollment policies, such as requesting proof of residency in the school district, as well as policies that may not be used by schools to deny enrollment to your child.

Proof of Residency in the School District

School officials may request proof that you live within the boundaries of the school district. School districts typically accept a variety of documents for this purpose, such as copies of phone or water bills, lease agreements, affidavits, or other important documents. A school district's requirements to establish residency must be applied in the same way for all children.

A school district may not ask about you or your child's citizenship or immigration status to establish residency within the district, nor may a school district deny a homeless child (including a homeless child who is undocumented) enrollment because he or she cannot provide the required documents to establish residency.

While a school district may choose to include a parent's state-issued identification or driver's license among the documents that can be used to establish residency, a school district may not require such documentation to establish residency or for other purposes where such a requirement would unlawfully bar a student whose parents are undocumented from enrolling in school.

Proof of Age

School officials may request documentation to show that a student falls within the school district's minimum and maximum age requirements. School districts typically accept a variety of documents for this purpose, such as a religious, hospital, or physician's records of birth or certificate showing date of birth; an entry in a family Bible; an adoption record; an affidavit from a parent; a birth certificate; or previously verified school records.

Although a school district might request documents such as those listed above to verify your child's age, a school district may not prevent or discourage your child from enrolling in or attending school because he or she lacks a birth certificate or has records that indicate a foreign place of birth, such as a foreign birth certificate.

Social Security Numbers

Some school districts request a student's social security number during enrollment to use as a student identification number. If a school district requests a student's social security number, it must: (1) inform you and your child that providing it is voluntary and that refusing to provide it will not bar your child from enrolling in or attending school, and (2) explain for what purpose the number will be used.

A school district may not prevent your child from enrolling in or attending school if you choose not to provide your child's social security number.

A school district may not require you to provide your own social security number in order for your child to enroll in or attend school.

Race or Ethnicity Data

School districts have some federal and state obligations to report race and ethnicity data about the students in their schools. A school district may request that you provide your child's race or ethnicity for this purpose.

However, a school district may not bar your child from enrolling if you choose not to provide your child's race or ethnicity.

If you want to learn more about your rights and the rights of your child when enrolling in public school, or if you believe that a school district is violating Federal Law, you may contact the following government agencies:

Department of Justice, Civil Rights Division, Educational Opportunities Section Telephone: (877) 292-3804 (toll-free) Fax: (202) 514-8337 Email: education@usdoj.gov

Department of Education, Office for Civil Rights Telephone: (800) 421-3481 (toll-free) Email: ocr@ed.gov If you wish to fill out a complaint form online with the Department of Education, you may do so at http://www.ed.gov/ocr/complaintintro.html

Department of Education, Office of the General Counsel Telephone: (202) 401-6000 Fax: (202) 205-2689

References:

U.S. Department of Justice Civil Rights Division

U.S. Department of Education Office for Civil Rights Office of the General Counsel

CHAPTER 18

CIVIC AFFAIRS ENGAGEMENT

"Ask not what your country can do for you-ask what you can do for your country." – John F. Kennedy

I came across the article whose objective is to encourage immigrants and members of refugee community who have become U.S. citizens to get involved in civic affairs. I learned a lot from Evangeline Kirigua, who authored the article entitled *Civic Engagement*, which I adopted to form the bulk of this chapter. I hope you get to learn from it as much as I did.

She is a fellow Kenyan, and I will let her introduce herself before diving into this important subject.

My name is Evangeline Kirigua. I live in Gaithersburg, Maryland. I was born in Kenya and have lived in the United States close to twenty years now. A few years ago, I became concerned that a lot of naturalized Americans are not involved in their civic affairs. As you all know, there are various ways that one can get involved, such as joining neighborhood associations, Parents' Teachers Associations (PTAs), and voting in elections.

Here we go:

I break this topic into 4 sections to help with the flow of the concepts that I share with you.

Vision: To reach foreign-born nationals (naturalized citizens), their children, as well as Lawful Permanent Residents (LPRs). The goal is to inform them of the importance of being registered to vote. As a U.S. citizen, it is one's right and privilege to vote. With this goal in mind, I formed the Diaspora Initiative for Civic Engagement (DICE).

Time: 2020 is a presidential election year. There are primaries that are due in certain states.

Policies: Everything that takes place around us depends on policy. Policies are made by people, for people. They are made by people who show up at the table. Therefore, it is important to know who we vote into office and what they stand for.

Nature of outreach: There are three approaches in the electoral process. These are:

- Partisan: pertaining to a specific (political) party.
- Bipartisan: refers to two parties.
- Non-partisan: Not tied to any political party.

Who may be registered: Every citizen who is at least sixteen years old.

Who may vote: Citizens who are eighteen years old.

How & when to vote: One can vote in primary (local) elections: for congressional and state representatives, governors, county and municipal representatives.

Types of Primaries

- **Open Primary**: one can vote regardless of their party affiliation.
- **Closed Primary**: One can only vote for the party which they are affiliated with.

Each state uses one of these two systems; it is important to know which one your state uses.

Presidential Election: Anyone can vote regardless of their party affiliation.

Your vote is crucial: For every single vote not cast, the other side wins one vote by default. When one stays home and fails to cast their vote, they are effectively giving away a free vote. Think of this as a soccer match. When a team fails to show up for a match, the one that shows up for the game wins by default. This is why your vote is important. Our life depends on it.

Voting day: It is always the 1st Tuesday after the 1st Monday in November. Plan to avail yourself to vote. If you cannot make it on that day, plan ahead for early voting. It is always provided for and may be on Saturday and Sunday. There is no excuse for one not to vote.

Volunteering: To help achieve this monumental goal, one can volunteer with the Board of Elections in your county and state. You will receive a short orientation to help you get started.

I hope you will heed the call and start planning how you will be involved in the upcoming election.

CHAPTER 19

VOLUNTEER OPPORTUNITIES

"The best way to find yourself is to lose yourself in the service of others"
– Gandhi

Many of the resource centers and community agencies including nonprofits and local religious organizations that we have discussed in this book or others you might learn about (contact to see what they have available in terms of helpful resources, supports and tools) depend on volunteers to help provide services. As an immigrant or a member of refugee community, you can become part of the volunteering team in your local community by contacting one of your favorite agency, or one that offers a service that you have benefited from. You can also volunteer in one that utilizes skills that you are good at. That way, you can use volunteerism as an opportunity not only to serve others but to enhance your own skills.

Your local free medical and dental clinic, your food bank including local veterans and refugee non-profit organizations and the homeless shelter are good examples of programs that utilize volunteers offering diverse skills and experience.

Remember, all levels of volunteering are welcome including professionals, such as physicians, dentists, nurse practitioners and physician assistants. Many other volunteer positions are available, including interpreters, phlebotomists, receptionists and support staff. If you are comfortable doing it go ahead and check them out and see what opportunities exist for doing good in your own community.

For more information about all volunteer opportunities, contact each agency directly by visiting their website to get their contacts or to complete an online application.

I challenge you the same way I challenge every other immigrant and members of refugee community to contribute in some way to the public good in your own area of influence wherever you are. This is because in so doing, you will benefit immensely in so many ways as a human being.

CONCLUSION

Be Connected.

It's your future here in America and you're worth it. Find other entities and experts that are friendly to immigrants and tap into their resources and knowledge.

Tip: Your Congressman office has a lot of powers to assist you on various issues including immigration, domestic violence, jobs, school, visas for loved ones back home, etc. I have personally referred cases to these offices, so I know how helpful and effective the staff there can be.

Network with other immigrants. You can benefit immensely that way, by learning from them things like where jobs are and how to apply for them, where to find housing, where to find day care services that are affordable and cater for immigrants' needs, where to shop for ethnic food or some that are from your country of origin, including where to find affordable mechanics and legal services, etc.

Loneliness in America and what to do about it

I want to briefly revisit this topic and offer few suggestions

I believe being connected with others helps in many ways and coping with loneliness is one of them.

How does being connected with others help with loneliness?

See below for the answer expressed through my own thoughts and observation from working with hundreds if not thousands of immigrants both here in America and abroad.

One of the benefits of being connected is that it helps you to become part of a small community within a larger community. It gives you opportunities to have social connections which can greatly reduce loneliness, anxiety and depression. These problems and others can be caused by lack of social interactions.

In brief: most immigrants report that their lives in America eventually become easier after developing social connections and networking with other immigrants. They report this as greatly contributing to their adapting process to life in America.

So, make efforts to connect with others and learn few positive ways to add value in others because in the process of doing that, your own emotional problems will be addressed.

Also, if you want to be part of our community – which I recommend – and reap the benefits of being a member of our community, see below how to join.

Sign up to receive updates and valuable news through our website.

Visit us on:

www.thesimpleinsights.com

Facebook: yourspeakout

X: yourspeakout

Send us an email: info@thesimpleinsights.com

You can also send us an email and request to be added to receive our newsletter.

Pass the word

Tell others about this information and become a channel of blessings to help another person.

Be Heard

Send us feedback to let us know what you think about the topics we have addressed. What would you want us to address in future publications? We want to share what is helpful to the majority of people, and so your suggestions are important to us.

Send us your feedback

Email your suggestion to us at:

info@thesimpleinsights.com

You can also write us at:

2150 James St # 5204 Coralville IA 52241

DISCLAIMER

This guidebook is intended for informational purposes only and cannot serve as a substitute for the information provided by the actual agencies providing services and offering resources. If you have questions or concerns on whether you are eligible to utilize resources in your community, please contact the agency offering them directly for clarification. Readers are advised to not use this publication as a substitute for the policies and protocols agreed to and followed by healthcare clinicians and institutions.

www.ingramcontent.com/pod-product-compliance
Lightning Source LLC
La Vergne TN
LVHW020654100826
845148LV00012B/2482

* 9 7 8 1 7 3 3 9 7 9 8 3 2 *